GOAL SETTING

The WorkSmart Series

GOAL SETTING

Susan B. Wilson

amacom

AMERICAN MANAGEMENT ASSOCIATION
THE WORKSMART SERIES

New York • Atlanta • Boston • Chicago • Kansas City • San Francisco • Washington, D.C.
Brussels • Toronto • Mexico City • Tokyo

This book is available at a special
discount when ordered in bulk quantities.
For information, contact Special Sales Department,
AMACOM, a division of American Management
Association,
135 West 50th Street, New York, NY 10020.

This publication is designed to provide accurate and authoritative information in regard to the subject matter covered. It is sold with the understanding that the publisher is not engaged in rendering legal, accounting, or other professional service. If legal advice or other expert assistance is required, the services of a competent professional person should be sought.

Library of Congress Cataloging-in-Publication Data

Wilson, Susan B.
  Goal setting / Susan B. Wilson.
      p.   cm.—(The WorkSmart series)
    ISBN 0-8144-7830-1
    1. Goal setting in personnel management.
2. Goal (Psychology)
I. Title.   II. Series.
HF5549.5.G6W55   1994
658.3'142—dc20   93-26060
                                           CIP

Printing number

10   9   8   7

To
Janet L. Hawkins

CONTENTS

PART III. EFFECTIVE GOAL SETTING AND MANAGEMENT SKILLS

PREFACE

"Out of control" is the way that many people describe their lives. What about you? Do you find yourself daydreaming about things that you would like to accomplish but don't? Do you find yourself stretched in too many directions by the demands made on you by others? Do you find that you are just tired of juggling your many roles and responsibilities? If you answered yes to at least one of these questions, then this book is for you.

In today's world, life is busier than ever. But often, in our pursuits, we seem unable to accomplish those goals that are the most meaningful to us. Our lives seem controlled by outside forces. Family, work, hobbies, community, and friends compete for our attention. And unclear expectations lead to misunderstandings, confusion, anger, and disappointment. Precious resources of time, money, and energy are wasted. With hundreds of choices facing us daily, what can be done to maximize the use of our valuable time?

Setting goals in a thoughtful, reasoned manner is one way to guarantee that you get the results you want. Establishing goals is a way to sort out the many choices confronting you. Using a process to set goals helps you prioritize the areas and activities that concern you. A systematic look at goals lends balance and perspective to the use of your resources.

Goals are directional signs for nearly all that we do. Our responsibilities often include reaching personal goals, working with others to reach specific goals, and pursuing goals established in our professional lives. And so, this book discusses goal setting from three perspectives.

Part I, Setting Personal Goals, is an overview of the goal-setting process. Chapter 1 provides ten criteria to use when establishing your goals. Utilizing these guidelines will help you set achievable goals that are significant to you. Chapter 2 identifies five potential obstacles that can block progress toward your goals. Unchecked, these obstacles sap your energy, your time, and your enthusiasm for goal achievement. Chapter 3 identifies eleven strategies to heighten the probability that you will reach your goals. These strategies offer practical, nearly guaranteed advice for getting where you want to go.

Part II, Effective Goal Setting and People Skills, considers the impact of communicating effectively with people in order to reach goals, yours as well as theirs. Chapter 4 discusses assertiveness and its value in communicating goals in a fair, honest, and mutually respectful way. The more effectively you express your needs, the more likely it is that others will understand them. And that increased understanding often leads to improved teamwork among people who must work together. Chapter 5 considers goal setting as it relates to others' behavior. How can you encourage other people to do what you want them to do? This chapter helps you set goals that identify clear expectations and specific consequences. Additionally, practical strategies are given for maximizing results by stimulating the help and efforts of others.

Part III, Effective Goal Setting and Management Skills, considers the relationship between goal setting and the classic management skills of priority setting, planning, delegating, and time management. These skills are effective only if you first establish relevant, clear goals as guideposts for using them. Once you set your goals, priority setting helps identify what needs to be done first. A method for setting priorities helps you determine which goals receive the greatest investment of your time and energy. Planning is a key to helping you become more effective. Many people do a good job, but what proportion do a good job of what is most important and most needs to get done? Chapter 7, Planning, identifies specific action steps to take in order to reach your goals. Do you know what it takes to get things done through other people? Chapter 8 identifies delegation as a key skill. When your performance is judged by the goals that you achieve through the efforts of others, you need the strategies to effectively guide them. Chapter 9 considers time management. This chapter provides valuable tips and practical strategies to make the most of your time—a vital resource.

Be your own catalyst for making the needed changes to achieve more of your goals. This book is an exciting road map for helping you regain control of the way that you invest your time, energy, and talents. Enjoy the journey!

PART

I

SETTING PERSONAL GOALS

CHAPTER 1

GETTING STARTED

WHY BOTHER WITH GOAL SETTING?

Goal setting—turning dreams into achievements

Have you ever wondered why some people seem to have the ability to accomplish a lot? They know where they are headed and exude an enviable confidence. Effective goal setting is one of their keys to success. You may be working very hard at what you do, but without setting goals you'll find that your hard work doesn't yield meaningful results.

Remember *Alice in Wonderland*? At one point in the story Alice stops at the crossroads to ask the Cheshire Cat which road to take. He responds by asking where she wants to go. When she tells him that she "doesn't much care where," he replies, "then it doesn't matter which way you go." As a result, she wanders aimlessly in her travels.

Like Alice, we often travel the road of life without a specific direction or goal. Few of us make goal setting a priority. In fact, studies have shown that most people either do not know what they want from life or, if they do, have no plans for realizing their dreams. Only a small percentage of people have specific, well-defined goals. And people who most frequently reach their goals are those who write them down and develop the plans to reach them.

Take a moment to consider why writing down your goals makes such a significant difference in ultimate performance. Why do you think that writing down one's goals is so important?

If your response included the idea that goal achievers record their goals so that they can read them, absorb them, and plan for them, then you are on the right track. People who achieve their goals take an active role in achieving them. They write them down, and then plan for their achievement. This chapter considers ten guidelines for evaluating and writing down your goals. If you follow these guidelines, you will establish your goals in a way that nearly guarantees your effort will be rewarded. Time and again, your reward is successful goal achievement.

"If you don't know where you are going, you'll probably end up someplace else."

—YOGI BERRA

Before learning the ten guidelines for effective goal setting, take a few minutes to identify two of your goals—they can be anything as long as they are meaningful to you—and write them down. Then, complete the self-audit, which identifies ten elements for effective goal setting. Evaluate the extent to which you use these ideas when developing your goals.

Your Goals

1. _____

2. _____

Now complete the self-audit on page 5 by checking either "Nearly Always," "Sometimes," or "Rarely" for each statement.

TEN GUIDELINES THAT REALLY WORK

The questions you just answered identify ten guidelines for effective goal setting. Using these ideas ensures that you establish goals that can be accomplished. The ten guidelines are:

1. *Effective goals are written.* Many of us daydream about what we would like to accomplish. But how many of us pick up a pen and write down those things we most want to achieve? Once a dream is committed to paper, it becomes

SELF-AUDIT FOR GOAL SETTING

	Nearly Always	Sometimes	Rarely
1. When I set a goal, I write it down.	_____	_____	_____
2. I describe my goal in specific, measurable terms.	_____	_____	_____
3. I often visualize my goals.	_____	_____	_____
4. My goals are achievable.	_____	_____	_____
5. I set realistic deadlines for completing my goals.	_____	_____	_____
6. I break a large goal into manageable units.	_____	_____	_____
7. I look for the potential problems that may keep me from reaching my goals.	_____	_____	_____
8. I take action to remove or minimize those potential problems.	_____	_____	_____
9. I review progress toward my goals on a regular basis.	_____	_____	_____
10. I know the personal rewards of reaching my goals.	_____	_____	_____

Assess your responses by counting the number of times you responded "Nearly Always" and multiply that number by 3. Multiply the number of times you responded "Sometimes" by 2, and the number of time you responded "Rarely" by 1. Then add the resulting three numbers for a total score.

Nearly Always _____ (number of responses) × 3 = _____
Sometimes _____ (number of responses) × 2 = _____
Rarely _____ (number of responses) × 1 = _____

GRAND TOTAL = _____

(continues)

Analyzing Your Score

Score of:

24–30	Excellent job of setting effective goals. If you find that you do an excellent job of setting goals, but you feel you could be more successful in reaching them, then Chapter 2 may be especially meaningful for you.
18–24	You are on your way to achieving effective goal setting. Take another look at the statements where your responses were less than "Nearly Always": These are the areas for additional concentration.
Below 18	There are several areas in which you can improve your goal setting. In setting the goal of reading and using this book, you are becoming a more effective goal setter.

concrete. Your dream is given a sense of reality. Writing down your goals is a first step toward achieving them.

2. *Effective goals are written in specific, measurable terms.* If you write your goal in specific terms, then you probably have expressed it in a measurable way. A goal needs to be measurable so that your progress can be evaluated and so that you will know when you have achieved your goal. For instance, you may think about learning a new computer software package. But only when you describe your goal as "taking a class in WordPerfect between March and June and spending 6 to 8 hours a week to learn its applications to my job" will you have a definable, measurable goal.

> **"Goals are dreams with a deadline."**
>
> —BRIAN TRACY, AUTHOR OF *The Psychology of Success*

EXAMPLES OF MEASURABLE GOALS

- **By April 1, I will have my taxes completed and ready to be mailed.**
- **This week I will make fifteen sales calls and close on four of them.**
- **We will hire a new secretary within two weeks.**

3. *Effective goals can be visualized*. Picture yourself reaching your goal. Picture the result, the moment, and your feelings. Much of our energy for reaching goals comes from a desire to attain them. Usually, the more you desire something, the harder you will work toward achieving it. For example, a sales rep has won several awards. He accomplishes his extraordinary sales goals by visualizing his award of receiving the plaque and winning the trip each year. He says, "I can see myself walking across the stage, being congratulated by the CEO, and enjoying my moment in the spotlight. When I'm having a slow day, I just visualize the result that I want, and it renews my energy."

> "If my mind can conceive it and my heart can believe it, then I can achieve it."
>
> —MUHAMMAD ALI

Victor Frankl is a Viennese psychologist and survivor of a World War II concentration camp. In his book *Man's Search for Meaning*, Frankl describes people who were able to visualize their goals for living and, consequently, were able to withstand the tortures of their circumstances. He maintains that people who had no purpose died quickly; those who kept an eye on their goals were more likely to survive.

4. *Effective goals are achievable*. Goals need to challenge your skills and abilities, without discouraging your effort and performance. For example, when initially implementing a quality management program, companies do not usually target the highly acclaimed and highly competitive Malcolm Baldrige National Quality Award as their first goal. Instead, they establish less stringent quality goals at first so that work teams can experience success in reaching those more realistic goals. As competency, success, and confidence grow, work teams may then decide to stretch for the higher goal.

5. *Effective goals have realistic deadlines*. Goals need a schedule. You are more likely to take action when you set a realistic time frame for accomplishing your goal. Schedule enough time to reach the goal, but not so much time that

By identifying and taking action on potential problems, you can feel confident about future opportunities rather than anxious about future threats.

you lose interest in it. How many people have you heard say they need a vacation from their work but don't get around to taking one? A far higher percentage of people meet their goal when they record their specific intentions. "I will plan a vacation for the second week in March and arrangements will be settled by January 15."

6. *Effective goals are manageable.* Sometimes a goal can seem overwhelming because of its size. But if it is divided into smaller components, then it becomes easier to manage and is achievable. To hear your boss say that he wants you to open seventy-two accounts this year may sound unrealistic, but if you think of it in terms of six accounts each month, then the goal is more manageable.

7. *Effective goals are analyzed for their potential problems.* As you establish a goal, consider the steps you must take to accomplish it. Analyze the goal for potential problems that might keep you from reaching it. If a goal initially is considered in terms of what could go wrong, then you can take action to resolve or minimize problems before they occur. Critical thinking helps you cover all the angles and stay on the path toward achieving your goal.

ANALYZE YOUR GOAL FOR POTENTIAL PROBLEMS

What could go wrong with the goal of "Meeting a Project Deadline"?

1. A member on the project team does not complete his part on time.
2. A needed piece of equipment may break down (i.e., word processor).
3. Unexpected tasks related to the project may arise.
4. Supervisor may not like the format of the final result.

8. *Effective goals require action to eliminate or minimize the consequences of potential problems*. This is the follow-through for identifying potential problems. At this point you identify the *action* that is required to either remove the cause of the problem or minimize its consequences. For example, an unproductive team member could be the cause of a potential problem. Eliminate the problem by removing the unproductive member from the team. Other potential problems, however, can be dealt with only by minimizing their impact. For example, in manufacturing there is often a potential for equipment breakdown. Minimize the consequences by providing regular maintenance or having backup equipment available.

9. *Effective goals include a regular review of progress*. A periodic review of your goals will help ensure that they continue to be realistic, timely, and relevant. Consider, for example, the human resources director who, only twelve credit hours and a dissertation away from her doctorate, decided to quit. How could she invest the time, money, and energy to get so far toward a goal and then quit? After serious review of her career, family, and financial goals, she realized that the degree did not hold the promise it once had. Obtaining a doctorate was no longer a relevant goal for her life circumstances and interests.

10. *Effective goals yield rewards that are of value to you*. We stay motivated to work toward our goals when we know and desire the resulting rewards, whatever they may be. As you establish each goal, identify at least one meaningful reward for yourself. It may be money, recognition, a day off, or the quiet pleasure you feel for a job done well. Your reward can be anything of value to you, something that motivates your effort to accomplish the goal. Without recognizing specific benefits that accrue as a result of your efforts, the probability of reaching that goal decreases.

With these ten points in mind, review the two goals you wrote on page 4. Consider the extent to which you use the ten guidelines just discussed.

Which of the guidelines are the most difficult for you to use?

_____

_____

_____

_____

Keeping the guidelines in mind, how would you rewrite your goals?

_____

_____

_____

_____

Goals provide direction for your life; they focus your activities. Goals are the points on your road map where you can apply your talents and energies. Without well-constructed goals, your life is governed by whim or the urgency of the moment. But effective goals will provide you with the internal control to make things happen the way you want them to.

DO YOUR GOALS SHOW YOU THE WAY?

At the beginning of this chapter, you listed two goals to jump-start your thinking. Then you were given ten guidelines to help you consider those goals in a more systematic way. For the next exercise, review the areas of life listed below for which effective goal setting is critical. Check those areas for which you already have significant goals. Then write down those goals using the worksheet. If you need to, refer to the goal-setting guidelines to help you stay on track.

Life Areas

Place a check mark by those areas in which you want to write goals.

Spiritual ____

Personal development ____

Leisure time ____

Professional ____

Civic/community ____

Family ____

Social ____

Health/physical well-being ____

Educational ____

Financial ____

Other _____

_____

_____

Goals Worksheet

Life Area _____

Goals

1. _____
2. _____
3. _____

Life Area _____

Goals

1. _____
2. _____
3. _____

Life Area _____

Goals

1. _____
2. _____
3. _____

Life Area _____

Goals

1. _____
2. _____
3. _____

Life Area _____

Goals

1. _____
2. _____
3. _____

Life Area _____

Goals

1. _____
2. _____
3. _____

CHAPTER 2

POTENTIAL OBSTACLES TO REACHING YOUR GOALS

I'm on the right track, what's stopping me?

Suppose you know what you want, and you are on the right track to accomplishing your goals. Without warning, you suddenly face an obstacle that blocks your progress. And then it is difficult to remain focused and energetic. If you do nothing about the obstacles that arise, they can sap your energy, your time, and your enthusiasm. Consider the following list of obstacles that could block *you* from accomplishing your goals:

- I need to feel secure.
- I may fail.
- I doubt my skills.
- Changing the way I do things is not easy.
- I have too many things to do.

Each of these is a potential barrier you set up yourself to defeat your effort. But there are strategies for removing them—or at least for minimizing their impact.

I NEED TO FEEL SECURE

Many of us fear that, if we try something new, we may lose our sense of security. We enjoy the security of life as we know it. The irony is that this security can change at a moment's notice.

A major layoff at work, a storm that destroys your community, a personal tragedy—these events can put your security at risk and quickly alter your life. You don't have the power to control all the elements that can potentially affect you. So, a more dependable course of action is to build an internal security system within yourself. Instead of trying to grasp at an intangible security that could change momentarily, develop the coping skills that are so essential for life in a world of probable changes. Effective coping skills usually include the ability to handle stressful events, the ability to take calculated risks, and the ability to manage problems as they arise. An internal security system, built through effective coping skills, will help you make reasoned choices. You will find that the fear of giving up security will diminish as an obstacle to your success.

If you always play it safe, how will you ever get anywhere?

A middle manager who enjoyed the security of a hefty paycheck and company benefits also faced the strain of a dead-end job. His daily work lacked challenge, and it was not likely he would receive another promotion. He decided to weigh the merits of continuing in a secure but lackluster job versus the risk of seeking new challenges. After a six-month job search, he found a position that was a better fit with his talents and interests. And in the process, he developed the internal strengths of initiative, confidence, and improved interviewing skills. Just three months into his new position, he learned that several middle management positions, including his former position, had been eliminated at his former employer. For him, this was a lesson in how quickly one's perceived security can change, and how important it is to develop the personal strength to cope with life's changing circumstances and inherent risks.

Are you willing to give up some of your perceived security to accomplish a goal? If not, why not?

_____

_____

Do you agree that to "not change a thing" can be a risk? Why?

_____

_____

Which of your goals seems risky? Why?

_____

_____

Thinking About Risk

There are several ways to increase your level of comfort and manage the perceived risk associated with meeting one of your goals:

1. Specify the risk you associate with the particular goal under consideration. Identify how large that risk really is. If its potential impact is low, then rational thought suggests that the risk is minimal.

2. Determine the probability of that risk occurring. Is it very likely, somewhat likely, or not very likely at all? Unless the probability of occurrence is fairly high, your energy and time are better spent addressing higher-risk issues.

3. Identify the benefits that accrue from taking the risk and succeeding. After you determine the probability and degree of the risk, you may decide that the anticipated benefits outweigh the potential disadvantages.

4. Once you identify the probability and impact of the risk, and the benefits from pursuing the goal, there may be added advantage of seeking input from a friend or adviser.

> Several years ago, the new president of a company that manufactures plastics established a goal that had a low probability of serious risk but large potential financial benefits. The company wanted to sell polyurethane products to the oil and gas industry. Unfortunately, following the company's investment of $500,000 into the proposed product, the oil industry collapsed unexpectedly, and the investment was lost. Although it was a calculated risk, the company's president maintains that he used the failure as a learning opportunity. Instead of bemoaning his loss, he turned to his internal security system. He used well-honed problem-solving and stress-management skills to learn from the situation. As a result, he found other opportunities to pursue, and he maintained his ability to take other risks that have led to profitable products.

I MAY FAIL

When is the last time you failed at something? Was it truly a failure or were you able to learn from the situation? No one enjoys the feeling of failure, but often we are overly critical and extra-hard on ourselves. And once we feel that we have failed, we replay the incident in our mind until we view ourselves as failures instead of having one failed goal. If you fail to reach a goal, view the situation objectively. Avoid harboring negative emotions and feelings. Instead, identify what went well and what could have been done better. Identify opportunities to apply what you learned.

In trying to avoid failure, you may miss the adventure of personal growth, the fun of meeting a new challenge, or the excitement of living for those things in which you believe. Abraham Lincoln and Thomas Edison are examples of men who took risks and "failed" many times to reach their goals.

The fear of failure can keep you from discovering who you really are.

They used their failures as learning experiences, and were not deterred from continuing to set goals. Instead, each man held to a belief in himself as he continued to pursue the goals in which he so strongly believed.

Think for a moment about an experience that you consider a failure and write it down.

_____

_____

What feelings did you have about it?

_____

_____

Did the experience offer opportunities for personal growth? What were they?

_____

_____

Do you agree that you are better prepared for coping with the challenges of life for having had that experience?

_____

_____

Thinking About the Fear of Failure

Here are some ideas to help you reduce your fear of failure:

1. Confront your fear of failure. Why do you feel this way? Is this particular fear justified? If it is, what can you do to eliminate or reduce your fear?

2. Look at your failure from a new perspective. Failing to reach a goal does not make _you_ a failure. It only means that you did not reach that goal.

A promising junior executive at a blue-chip corpo-
ration lost several million dollars of that company's money in a new venture. The company's
president and founder summoned the executive
to his office. Trembling, he stood in front of the
president and said, "I guess you want my resig-
nation." Without hesitation, the president replied,
"You can't be serious. We've just spent millions of
dollars educating you." This rising star was being
reminded of the opportunity to learn from failure
and to use the experience as a springboard for
renewed effort toward company goals.

3. Working toward a goal includes taking specific steps.
Although you may fail to reach the goal, there are benefits
of having worked toward it. One benefit is the practical
education of making the effort. Another is the opportunity
to practice specific skills. A third is the recognition that
meeting some goals and failing to meet others is part of the
ebb and flow of life.

4. Recognize that you probably will not achieve significant goals without some failures. Failing provides unique
learning opportunities that ultimately contribute to your
personal growth and to your organizational contribution.

I DOUBT MY SKILLS

Do you have a strong commitment to reaching your goals?
If not, this lack of commitment may weaken your confidence
in your own skills and abilities. You think to yourself, "I
think I can do this, but I'm really not sure." Since the
manner in which you mentally talk to yourself impacts your
performance, it is important to focus on your strengths.
Identify your abilities in a positive way. Focus on the things
that you do well. Then decide which skills need work and
identify strategies for improving these. Taking positive spe-

An insurance company decided to apply for the Malcolm Baldrige National Quality Award. In that year, sixty-six companies competed. The company was judged as one of the two best service organizations in America, but it did not meet the goal of winning the National Award. Far from viewing their effort as a failure, employees celebrated their commitment to quality, appreciated what they had learned in the award process, and were grateful for the feedback regarding their quality improvement program.

cific action will help you develop confidence in your skills and abilities.

Do you lack confidence in your skill or ability to reach a goal? If yes, why?

_____

_____

What will you do to increase your confidence?

_____

_____

How will you renew a commitment to your goal?

_____

_____

Thinking About Increasing Your Confidence

Here are some ideas to help you build confidence in your skills and abilities:

Concentrate on your strengths and on your personal power.

1. Think specifically and positively about your skills and abilities. Identify how they can contribute to each of your goals. Write these down.

2. Keeping your skills and abilities in mind, establish a realistic standard of achievement for your goal.

3. Establish a step-by-step plan for reaching your goal so that you can mark your progress.

4. When trying something new, think in terms of specific skills or behaviors that need changing. Avoid generalizations. Instead of "I'm terrible at running a meeting," try "I need to develop and use an agenda."

5. Avoid the exclusive use of others' opinions when evaluating your skills. Include your beliefs and your opinions as you make decisions about changes that need to be made.

6. For each criticism that you give yourself, also give yourself one or two specific compliments.

CHANGING THE WAY I DO THINGS IS NOT EASY

Change often leads to personal growth.

Do you enjoy change? If so, you probably are in the minority. Change is uncomfortable for most of us, even when it is for the better. Change means letting go of what is familiar. When we do that, we face the challenge of coping with new ideas and situations. But as much as you may resist change, it cannot be stopped. Your challenge is to accept that change is inevitable, so that your resources are used in concert with that change. Working against change often can be stressful, while working with and through change is a source of energy and greater strength. When you strive toward new goals, often you must change in some way. If you view change as a catalyst for reaching those goals, you will be better able to accept change with a more grateful perspective.

Which of your most significant goals require you to change in some way?

_____

_____

In what ways do you need or want to change?

_____

_____

Thinking About Managing Change

Here are some ideas to help you face change:

1. If change is a problem, admit it. Often, a first step to dealing with a problem is to admit that it exists.

2. If possible, experience change gradually. Handling change all at once is tougher than easing into it. Many people find that they can even schedule the changes that they must accept.

3. Try seeking change as opposed to its seeking you. This will give you a sense of greater control over your future.

4. See yourself as someone who looks forward to change. Try new foods or new activities, and seek new acquaintances. Doing so establishes a pattern of willingness to experience the new.

I HAVE TOO MANY THINGS TO DO

Frequently, there *are* too many things to do. Fortunately, you have the ability to prioritize your goals and activities. Review your list of goals at the end of Chapter 1. Which are the most important to you? Which give you the greatest return on your investment? Which provide you with the greatest enjoyment or sense of accomplishment? Use your responses to prioritize the goals that are the most important to you. Then plan your hours, your days, and even your months to reach those goals.

In working on tasks, ignore the trivial and concentrate on the vital.

Thinking About Prioritizing Your Goals

The following steps will help you put your goals in order of priority:

1. Identify criteria for prioritizing your goals. For example, which are the most important to you? Which have the greatest impact?
2. Use a high-medium-low scale to assess your goals, using your criteria.
3. Those goals with the highest rankings are your high-priority items.

Most of us realize that effective goal setting is a key to getting things accomplished. However, as we have reviewed in this chapter, there are potential obstacles that impede progress. Only when you understand the nature of the obstacles confronting you can you develop strategies to minimize these and achieve your goals.

CHAPTER 3

ELEVEN STRATEGIES TO OPTIMIZE REACHING YOUR GOALS

Although reaching your goals cannot be guaranteed, raise the probability of achieving them with the eleven strategies discussed in this chapter.

Before reading on, review the boxed questions on the next page and mark your responses. Then score yourself using the information that follows the questions.

KNOW THE RESOURCES REQUIRED FOR REACHING A GOAL

Personal desire for reaching a goal is powerful, but often other resources are needed as well. What resources do you need to reach your goals—time, money, position? Additional education? The help of a particular person?

For example, consider the goal of purchasing a computer system for your home office. The resources you might need include: money to purchase the computer, the software, and the printer; additional knowledge for knowing how to use it; and the help of a computer consultant.

Now, consider one of your goals. What specific resources are needed for its achievement?

Goal: _____

Resources Required: _____

_____

ELEVEN STRATEGIES FOR GOAL SETTING

	Often	Sometimes	Rarely/ Never
1. I know what resources I need to reach my goals.	_____	_____	_____
2. I work toward goals that are compatible with one another.	_____	_____	_____
3. I am comfortable asking for help to reach my goals.	_____	_____	_____
4. I accept the responsibility for working toward my goals.	_____	_____	_____
5. I minimize interruptions that get in the way of reaching my goals.	_____	_____	_____
6. I am flexible to changes that affect my progress toward my goals.	_____	_____	_____
7. I know the benefits of reaching my goals.	_____	_____	_____
8. I am persistent about working toward my goals.	_____	_____	_____
9. I review my progress toward my goals on a regular basis.	_____	_____	_____
10. I achieve a balance of effort between the goals that are important to me.	_____	_____	_____
11. I only pursue those activities that are related to reaching my goals.	_____	_____	_____

Assess your responses to this exercise by counting the number of times that you responded "Often" and multiply that number by 3. Multiply the number of times that you responded "Sometimes" by 2, and the number of times that you responded "Rarely/Never" by 1. Then add the resulting three numbers for a total score.

Often   _____(number of responses) × 3 = _____
Sometimes   _____(number of responses) × 2 = _____
Rarely/Never   _____(number of responses) × 1 = _____

                                    Grand Total = _____

Analyzing Your Score

Score of:

33–39   You have a healthy understanding of what it takes to see your goals accomplished.

26–32   You are well on your way to developing the personal discipline for reaching your goals.

19–26   You will find the information in this chapter useful as you sharpen the skills for reaching your goals.

Strategies for Staying Power

The statements to which you responded relate to strategies that encourage your "staying power" when working toward a goal. Most of us benefit from strategies that strengthen our resolve. Each of these strategies is discussed in detail in this chapter. As you read, note your areas of strength as well as opportunities for improvement.

WORK WITH GOALS THAT ARE COMPATIBLE

When goals conflict with one another they compete for your time, energy, and personal resources, which can leave you feeling drained and stressed. For example, a manager was challenged by his boss to spend more time on the production floor interacting with his employees, and then was criticized for not spending enough time at his desk. To him, these two goals were in conflict with one another.

Another example is the manager who wanted to complete her doctorate. She enrolled at a university and was beginning her studies when she learned that she was pregnant. In analyzing the situation, she discovered that the goals of pursuing an education, maintaining a full-time job, and starting a family were not compatible at that time. Trying to meet the challenges of these goals would deplete her resources of energy, time, and enthusiasm.

Review your goals. Which ones are competing for your resources? How can you modify or change your goals so that they are more compatible?

_____

_____

BE WILLING TO ASK FOR HELP WITH YOUR GOALS

Many people are willing to help you if you ask for their assistance. Specify your needs and identify specific ways in which others can help. Remember, part of the way you can repay the help you receive is to be a resource for others.

Whose skills, knowledge, and/or gifts can help you reach one or more of your goals?

_____

_____

Which of your skills, knowledge, and/or gifts can you use to help someone else?

_____

_____

ACCEPT THE RESPONSIBILITY FOR DOING THE WORK THAT IS NECESSARY TO REACH YOUR GOALS

Establishing goals is a start. Accepting the responsibility to accomplish them is another challenge. When the going gets tough, many people begin to blame others for their lack of progress. Instead of getting caught in a defensive, blaming trap, apply your time and energy to solving problems, making decisions, and working your plan so that your goals are realized.

How do you typically react when faced with a problem?

_____

_____

Does your reaction get in the way of your potential success?

_____

_____

Are you willing to change your behavior? If so, how?

_____

_____

Minimize the Interruptions That Block Your Progress Toward Your Goals

Many interruptions have the appearance of urgency and importance, but often they are time wasters and trivial matters. When an interruption arises, quickly evaluate it in terms of its importance to your goals. If it is not an enabler to your progress, then it may be a hindrance.

Do you control interruptions or do interruptions control you?

_____

_____

Do you handle interruptions swiftly and decisively?

_____

_____

What specific actions can you take to minimize the interruptions to your day?

_____

_____

Be Flexible to Changes That Affect Your Progress Toward a Goal

Although a planned path optimizes progress toward your goals, the unexpected does sometimes arise and can either impede or facilitate progress. When an unforeseen change in your plan occurs, evaluate it for damage control. Brainstorm alternatives to eliminate or minimize the impact of the problem, but also look for opportunities!

An advertising agency that was growing quickly felt several pressures affecting its progress toward its five-year goal of becoming known nationally for creative thinking. The company's president died unexpectedly, a multimillion-dollar account was lost, the economy forced several other clients to drop the services, and several key management people left the company. Instead of allowing these changes to debilitate the company, agency executives sought opportunities in the challenges. They streamlined the agency, recommitted themselves to a vision of what the agency could be, and sought outside assistance to strengthen skills.

What are the potential problems or changes that could get in the way of reaching one of your goals?

_____

_____

What actions will you take to optimize your opportunities and minimize potential problems?

Action to Optimize   Action to Minimize

_____   _____

_____   _____

IDENTIFY THE BENEFITS OF REACHING YOUR GOALS

Get tuned into WII–FM (What's In It For Me?). Knowing and wanting the goal's benefits is a key factor in motivating you to apply your time, energy, and resources. No salesperson is successful without an effort to sell the benefits of a product or a service to the client. So sell your goal's benefits to yourself. Perhaps the benefits include exposure to upper management, a chance to learn something new, or the opportunity for a promotion. When you value the benefit that you'll receive, that value increases your motivation to reach the goal.

What factors motivate you to work toward a particular goal?

_____

_____

What are the benefits of reaching one or more of your goals?

_____

_____

DEVELOP THE PERSISTENCE TO WORK TOWARD YOUR GOALS

Persistence may be the most important quality for reaching your goals. Many people are willing to quit when the going gets rough. What about you? Are you willing to make short-term sacrifices in order to accomplish something that is meaningful to you?

Consider your goals. On a scale of 1 to 10 (10 = high), how important are your goals to you?

_____

_____

If you believe that they are important, do you have the persistence to work toward your goals?

_____

_____

REVIEW YOUR PROGRESS TOWARD YOUR GOALS REGULARLY

Reviewing your goals not only identifies the progress you've made, but also provides an opportunity to ensure that you are on track and that you have adequate resources at your disposal. A review of your goals also fans the fire of motivation by highlighting your accomplishments. Consider posting a list of your goals so you can see them on a daily basis. Charting your progress regularly is also motivating.

Do you make a point of reviewing your goals on a regular basis?

_____

_____

Would charting your progress increase your motivation?

_____

_____

BALANCE YOUR EFFORT AMONG THE GOALS THAT ARE IMPORTANT TO YOU

Often we find ourselves applying a disproportionate amount of time to certain goals. One successful realtor who sold $7 million dollars' worth of real estate in a year realized that while she said that her family was very important to her, in reality she did not share much of her time and energy with them. Instead, most of her resources went to her job. Those long hours might ensure job performance, but goals related to other areas of life (family, friends, community, or spiritual life) may suffer.

In Chapter 1 you identified goals related to different areas of your life. Do you apply adequate resources of time, energy, and resources to each of those areas that are important to you? If not, what changes are you willing to make?

_____

_____

REACH YOUR GOALS BY CONCENTRATING ON THOSE THINGS THAT RELATE TO YOUR GOALS

Whatever activities are planned in your day, consider their value to reaching your goals. Frequently, there are activities that you can eliminate or modify so that you can concentrate on making progress toward your significant goals.

Are you willing to give priority to those activities that contribute specifically to your goals? How can you do this?

_____

_____

Experiencing progress toward goals that are meaningful to you is gratifying and can motivate you toward even more accomplishments. Using these eleven strategies nearly guarantees progress toward reaching your goals. Prepare to reap the benefits of your effort!

PART

EFFECTIVE GOAL SETTING AND PEOPLE SKILLS

CHAPTER 4

ASSERTIVE BEHAVIOR

**Become the cata-
lyst for
making
good things
happen to
yourself.**

How often have you felt frustrated by a difficulty to express yourself clearly and concisely? Have you tried to express your goals to a colleague and then realized that your colleague didn't understand you? Do you wish that you could communicate more effectively? By being assertive, you convey your needs and goals in a clear and direct manner. Assertiveness is a communication style that confirms your right to be heard, but in a caring and respectful manner toward others. The more clearly and reasonably you express your goals, the more likely others will understand them. And as others understand your needs, they are more likely to help you attain your goals.

Assertiveness often is misunderstood. Frequently the word conjures up an image of a meek person suddenly changed into a tough individual. A popular cartoon shows a man looking tentatively at a door labeled, "Assertiveness Training, Barge Right In." Although funny, the cartoon illustrates the dilemma concerning assertiveness: People often associate assertive behavior with aggressive behavior.

Assertive behavior is an honest expression of your opinions, feelings, and beliefs. It is behavior that demonstrates your right to be treated with dignity and respect. Assertiveness is evidenced through your words, behavior, and actions. For example, imagine that you are one of ten participants at a meeting scheduled for 3:00 P.M. At 3:10 P.M., two of the participants have not yet arrived. Although you are not the chairperson, you want the meeting to start so as to: (1) minimize the cost of wasted time, (2) have the opportunity

Assertiveness stresses mutuality: I respect and try to uphold your rights, as well as my own.

to contribute to the meeting, and (3) leave by 4:00 P.M. so that you can get to your 4:10 appointment on time. Instead of staying quiet and inwardly fuming, you say to the chairperson, "It's 3:10. Since most of us are here let's get started so that we can finish on time." Your statement raises the probability of achieving your goals while at the same time respects the time of others.

Honesty regarding your thoughts, opinions, and feelings is integral to assertive behavior, but so is showing respect and concern for others. The key difference between assertiveness and aggressiveness is that the assertive person accepts others' needs and goals while the aggressive person does not.

There are no absolute guidelines for cultivating assertive behavior. However, there are a number of ways you can work on this skill:

1. *Practice, practice, practice.* Communication is dynamic. New situations, new people, varied moods, and deeper insights challenge your ability to communicate honestly, clearly, and respectfully. Begin to flex your assertive behavior in nonthreatening, low-risk situations. Consider, for example, your need to confront two situations at work. The first involves a co-worker who consistently leaves your computer on after she borrows it. The other is your boss, who either yells or gives you the cold shoulder when a mistake occurs. Which situation would *you* choose to deal with first? Probably the forgetful co-worker, in order to build a reservoir of successfully using assertive behavior. As you feel more confident with your assertiveness, you will be more effective when confronting riskier situations, such as an overbearing boss.

2. *Consider the situation.* Be aware of what is going on around you. For example, consider the salesperson who travels internationally to service his accounts. In the United States, it is assertive for him to be direct in his sales presentation. And it is assertive to ask for the sale at the close of the presentation. However, in Japan, this situation probably would be perceived very differently—directness is viewed as

pushy and aggressive. Japanese culture requires an emphasis on relationship and process. What is accepted as assertive behavior in the United States very likely is perceived as aggressive in Japan.

3. *Avoid hurting others.* "What a stupid idea" may be an honest expression of thought, but it has the potential of hurting the feelings of the other party. When you are in doubt about how your communication might be understood, ask yourself: "Would I feel comfortable if someone were talking to me in this way?" and "Is my communication honest and direct, but given in a caring manner?"

In a meeting, someone establishes a goal that you think is without merit. How do you express your view in an honest, but fair and respectful way?

---

4. *Treat everyone with respect and dignity.* An assertive person treats those involved in the communication process with respect and dignity because they are deserving of those rights as people, not because of an organizational hierarchy, a false sense of status, or a difference in credentials, background, or experiences. An assertive individual, whether speaking with a housekeeper or the president of a company, makes it a practice to treat people with courtesy and respect. Your attention to the dignity of all people empowers you to reach your goals. When you are recognized as someone who respects people, others are more willing to help you reach your goals because they believe that you will care about their goals as well.

Your assertive behavior encourages assertive behavior in others. If you behave in an open, honest, and direct manner, and treat others with dignity and respect, then people are likely to respond in the same way. Even when a confrontation is initially aggressive, your assertive response can guide the communication toward mutual honesty and respect. If the aggression continues in spite of your best efforts, however, an assertive response might be, "I can see that you are

Your personal power and influence increase when you choose an assertive style of behavior.

quite angry. We can reschedule this discussion when we both feel calmer.'' In doing so, you don't allow the other party to treat you in a less than respectful manner.

People who use their assertiveness skills report feeling an increased sense of personal power. They feel more confident, more likable, and more respected. Another outcome is that they are more likely to achieve their goals as well as contribute to the goals of others.

YOU HAVE A CHOICE

We operate on a behavioral continuum that is dynamic and that includes three kinds of behaviors: assertive, aggressive, and passive. Our movement along the continuum is affected by the situations in which we find ourselves. The environment, the mood, and the people involved affect the choices we make regarding our behavior. Optimally, assertive behavior is most frequently chosen. Neither the passive nor the aggressive style optimizes the achievement of goals. Passive behavior tends to defer to others. A person choosing this style treats others with respect, but doesn't expect others to return that respect—and therefore often they don't. Aggressive behavior, on the other hand, demands attention from others. People with an aggressive style expect respect from others and make their goals known, but they are insensitive to the goals and needs of others.

Consistent use of either the passive or the aggressive style increases the risk of alienating people and losing their support, which is critical to accomplishing goals. Developing assertive behavior is a habit that can be cultivated if you choose to do so. Let's look more closely at these three behavioral styles.

Passive Behavior

For many, passive behavior is a way to avoid conflict. The passive behavioral style suppresses personal needs in order to get along with others. It also avoids taking personal responsibility to establish and communicate goals. Passive behavior often includes rambling thoughts, apologetic words, indirect speech, and silence. People with a passive style hope that others can guess their needs. Goals, if reached, are accomplished in a random fashion because they are not expressed clearly and assertively.

A passive style demonstrates a lack of respect for one's own needs.

Over time, however, other people become frustrated trying to communicate with a passive person. The often unclear and ambiguous communication means that the listener interprets the information to meet his or her own needs. As a result, the passive person is easily hurt, disappointed, and even angry about interactions, and tends to avoid situations that seem risky or confrontational.

Describe a time when you chose to use a passive style of behavior.

_____

_____

How did you feel?

_____

_____

Did you accomplish your goal?

_____

_____

Aggressive Behavior

The person with an aggressive style expresses thoughts and feelings loudly and clearly, but often does not welcome that same honest expression from others. The person with aggressive behavior often demonstrates a loss of self-control as he or she demands control of a situation in order to meet goals. Anger, sarcasm, arrogance, and even outbursts are used. Situations are either win or lose, and the aggressive individual intends to emerge as the winner. An aggressive person is recognized by a tense demanding voice, narrowed staring eyes, rigid posture, and abrupt gestures. He or she may intimidate and accomplish goals in the short run; however, the anger and hostility that this behavior creates in others diminish the opportunities for accomplishing long-term goals.

Describe a time when you used aggressive behavior.

_____

_____

How did you feel?

_____

_____

How would you choose to handle a similar situation in an assertive way?

_____

_____

Assertive Behavior

Sending a message of acceptance, assertive behavior is expressive of personal wants and needs, but seeks that same expression from others, with a willingness to listen and understand. In this way, the assertive person is emotionally honest about equalizing the power in a relationship. The assertive person speaks in a personalized, direct manner. He or she tends to be persuasive because the interactions are honest, supportive, and clear.

Personal characteristics of assertiveness include a friendly, relaxed voice; eye contact; relaxed posture; and relaxed, open

You can only be responsible for your own behavior. But your behavior can impact the behavior of others.

gestures. This style is self-perpetuating in that it demonstrates warmth and respect for others and encourages the same. The assertive person embraces confidence, self-respect, and personal caring as well as caring for others. The ability to recognize and work for positive outcomes is an asset of the assertive person. Consequently, this is a person who frequently accomplishes personal goals.

If you decide to use an assertive style of communication more frequently, what will be the positive outcomes for you?

_____

_____

Frequently, your interactions with others are goal-related. You need to know how to communicate effectively with others so that they will start, stop, or keep doing those things that are helpful to you. Assertiveness provides a method for doing so by using communication that is honest, direct, and respectful.

Developing Assertive Messages

There are three components to delivering an effective assertive message:

1. Identify the real issue, and develop a specific description of the behavior.
2. Express your feelings about that behavior to the person who can take action.
3. Describe the positive or the negative consequences of that behavior.

For example, imagine that one of your colleagues is always late for meetings. By describing the behavior, the concern is more easily understood by your listener. For example, it is more specific to say, "You have been fifteen minutes late

ASSERTIVE RESPONSES

Read the following situations and identify each as an example of passive, aggressive, or assertive behavior. If you label the response as either passive or aggressive, write an assertive response.

1. *Situation*: There is one member of your project team who often interrupts you when you are speaking. You say: "You interrupt all of the time. Could you just hold on a minute?" _____
   Assertive response: _____ .

2. *Situation*: Your boss turns silent during a meeting with you and doesn't say what is on her mind. You say nothing about her silence. Instead, you rush on to finish what you are saying so that you can get out of her office. _____
   Assertive response: _____ .

3. *Situation*: You believe that you deserve a raise, but instead of seeing your supervisor about it you grumble about the large salaries of top management to your colleagues. _____
   Assertive response: _____

4. *Situation*: A joint management-union committee has been established to review the past year's safety performance. The time of the meeting is convenient for others but not for you. You know you will not be able to attend regularly. You say: "I would like to be part of this committee, but the meeting time will not work with my schedule. What other times would be convenient for all of us?" _____
   Assertive response: _____

5. *Situation*: An employee is making a lot of mistakes in his work lately. You say: "I've noticed that the quality of your work has dropped in the past two weeks. I'd like to know if you agree and what you want to do about it." _____
   Assertive response: _____

Here are potential answers.

1. *Aggressive.* Your goal may be to avoid interruptions while you are speaking. An assertive response is to say, "Excuse me, I would like to finish what I was saying and then you can give your comments."

2. *Passive.* One of your goals in this situation is to ensure that your boss is supportive of your position. If so, she needs to be encouraged to say what is on her mind rather than to remain silent. An assertive response might be for you to stop your presentation and say, "I've noticed that you haven't asked me many questions. Are there any questions or concerns that you want to express?"

3. *Passive.* Your goal may be to ask for a raise. If so, it is most direct to speak to your supervisor with prepared comments for why a raise is deserved. One assertive action is to schedule a meeting with your supervisor and initiate conversation by saying, "I'd like to discuss my performance and the potential of a raise with you."

4. *Assertive.* The goal of the situation is to contribute to the committee at a time that is convenient for all members.

5. *Assertive.* Your goal is to improve the quality of the employee's work.

three times this week" than to say, "You are always late." While you can time someone's appearance on the job, it is difficult to document that someone is "always late." Rarely are absolute words true. Words such as *always, never, totally, absolutely, every,* and *constantly* are best left unused unless you can document their accuracy.

Additionally, make sure you identify the *real* issue. How often have you complained about one thing when something else really was bothering you? Television situation comedies use this theme for laughs, but in real life it can lead to major problems in both professional and personal relationships. You might have an assertive message that sounds correct, but if you are not expressing the real issue, communication is blocked. For example, to complain about someone's tardiness when the real issue is work left incomplete leaves the real issue unresolved.

The second part of the assertive message deals with feelings that sometimes are difficult to describe. However, not discussing feelings can block honest communication. Expressing your feelings about how the behavior affects your needs and your goals provides additional information for those who work with you. Try identifying your true feelings; don't overstate or understate them. A colleague who tends toward the dramatic indicates that "something awful has happened" when the copier breaks down. On the other hand, a more stoic friend indicates that she is "unhappy" when she is laid off from her job. Neither expression of feeling seems appropriate for the event.

It's also crucial that your message is heard by the person who has the power to take action to resolve your concern. Asserting to anyone else will only sound like a complaint—and it also wastes time and energy that could be applied to correcting the situation.

The third component of the assertive message is to express the consequences of the behavior in question. Whether positive or negative, explaining the consequences provides a listener with more complete information. Understanding the consequences and how the behavior affects you may encourage your listener to adjust in a way that benefits you. Consider the example of establishing a mutually convenient meeting time for committee members. It is helpful for participants to understand the consequence of changing the meeting time: that the group will meet its goal of having input from each committee member. Knowing the consequences provides useful information as decisions are made.

How would you handle the following situations in an assertive way?

1　Your boss keeps adding projects to your work load. You'd like to discuss the situation. You say:

_____

_____

2. You are finding that several employees often come to you with work that you have assigned them to do. Although you don't mind assisting when needed, you believe that they could do a better job of researching and problem solving. What do you do?

_____

_____

3. Your office is shared with a co-worker. Both of you need frequent use of the computer, and you are having scheduling problems. Both of you seem to want to use it at the same time. What do you say?

_____

_____

Here are sample responses to each of the three situations:

1. "Suzanne, I would like to discuss my work load with you. As you probably know, I have a pretty full agenda, and I'd like to be sure that you and I are in agreement about my priorities. If not, I want to make the needed changes now."

2. "I don't mind assisting you if you have a specific question or concern. However, before you schedule time with me, please identify the purpose of the meeting, prepare to tell me of your progress to date in three to five minutes, and be specific in asking for my assistance. Keep in mind that this is your project; you are the project head. I expect to provide only a consulting perspective."

3. "John, I feel pretty frustrated about our scheduling conflicts over the use of the computer. We both seem to need

it at the same time. Let's meet for an hour this afternoon to see if we can work this out. I'll bring some of my ideas, and it would help if you would bring some of yours. This must be pretty frustrating for you, too, and I'd like to see the situation resolved for both of us."

Assertiveness is a skill that requires regular attention and practice for effective use. Although each of us makes choices about how and when we use this behavior, we build credibility when assertiveness is used consistently. Most people recognize respectful and honest communication as a strength. It is likely that your ability to reach your goals will dramatically improve if you "grow" your assertiveness skill. Treating others with dignity and respect is a gift they deserve; treating yourself with dignity and respect is a gift you give yourself.

BENEFITS OF ASSERTION

Assertive communication increases self-confidence.
Assertive communication reduces conflict.
Assertive communication demonstrates consideration and respectful behavior.
Assertive communication reduces stress.

CHAPTER 5

CHANGING PEOPLE'S BEHAVIOR

"The great thing in this world is not so much where we are, but in what direction we are moving."

—OLIVER WENDELL HOLMES

Effective goal setting is a key component to changing behavior—yours as well as others. When you ask someone to do something, you establish a goal for that person. And by setting a goal, you expect that person to behave in ways that lead to reaching that goal.

There are times when your goals mesh with the goals of others. But other times you will want to convince people to do something that you want done. What can you do to motivate others to work toward the goals you have set? How can you encourage others to understand your perspective? What can you do to change someone's behavior?

DEFINING BEHAVIOR

Since we emphasize behavior here, let's first define the word. For this discussion, *behavior* is a person's actions that are observable and that have a beginning and an end. However, your evaluation of someone's behavior often is biased by your experiences, judgments, and/or perceptions. A fair approach to evaluating behavior is to determine what specific results you want to see and observe those behaviors that lead to those results.

Examples of *nonbehavior*—or actions that cannot be measured and observed objectively in and of themselves—are courteousness, aggressiveness, neatness, and cheerfulness. What is judged as courteous by you may differ from what is viewed by one of your colleagues. What strikes you as cheerful may

47

Examples of behaviors that are measurable, observable, and time-bound are:
- **Completing paperwork correctly**
- **Thanking an employee**
- **Arriving at work by 8:00 A.M.**
- **Shouting at a co-worker**
- **Giving step-by-step work instructions**

be seen as aloof by your supervisor. How about the employee who rarely smiles? You might judge him as unfriendly simply because he is not a smiler. However, in getting to know him, you discover that he does smile and does behave in a friendly manner as he becomes more comfortable in the relationship. There is the realization that perhaps he is a shy person, not unfriendly.

Before making judgments about the behavior of others, ask yourself the following questions:

- Am I making a quick judgment based on my past experiences, feelings, and perceptions?
- Am I looking for specific behavior on which to evaluate this person?
- Am I am defining behavior by making observations that are measurable, observable, and time-bound (with a beginning and an end)?

UNDERSTANDING BEHAVIOR

Regardless of who we are, our actions are in response to a variety of motivations. Understand this, and you will understand human behavior. Use the following principles, and you will strengthen your ability to reach your goals through the efforts of others.

Your Behavior Affects the Way Others Behave

To change someone else's behavior, you may first have to change your own. For an example, see the box on page 50.

A Person Behaves in Ways That Seem Reasonable to That Person

In order to change behavior, you need first to accept that any behavior is rational and logical to the person exhibiting

Which of the following phrases is a behavior? Mark them with a *B*. Identify all nonbehaviors with an *N*.
1. Being rude ____
2. Picking someone up at 8:00 A.M. ____
3. Teaching a software package to a colleague ____
4. Seeking extra project assignments ____
5. Having an attitude problem ____
6. Being fairer to one work group than to another ____
7. Facilitating a meeting ____
8. Giving a good performance appraisal ____
9. Conducting a thirty-minute performance appraisal ____

Answers: 1. N
          2. B
          3. B
          4. B
          5. N
          6. N
          7. B
          8. N
          9. B

it because his or her goals may differ from yours. Additionally, each one of us behaves in ways that are based on our unique backgrounds and experiences. Thus, we frequently respond to what seems to be the same situation in different ways. For example, while working at a nuclear power plant in New York, an engineer heard a lot of talk about radiation and the need to limit exposure to it. The plant had a policy that stated a specific level of radiation exposure above which no employee of the plant should experience. Although most employees were sensitive to this issue and were committed to following the policy, there was one group that did not.

A manager had an employee who was chronically late for work. She tried several techniques for handling the situation—anger, jokes, silent treatment. One day, she realized that her "counseling" was filled with idle threats regarding the lateness. She needed to change and be more specific, and directly communicate a goal to the employee. She needed to establish a specific goal, describe the consequences of not reaching that goal, and then follow through with the consequences. And so she arranged a meeting with the employee and said, "I have been angry about your tardiness for several months and we have discussed it frequently. This is our final discussion before I take action. One of your goals is to report to work on time. This meeting constitutes a formal warning regarding your tardiness. The next time you are late, a note will be put into your file. If there is a next time after that, you will be suspended for three days without pay. For the next six months, on the basis of your past record, action against your tardiness will be taken regardless of the circumstances."

To some of the foremen, exceeding this level of exposure developed into a contest—behavior that probably would not seem rational to the outside observer. But it made sense to the foremen. Part of the culture of their group was to exceed the exposure limit in order to prove to their peers how "macho" they were.

If Behavior Leads to Positive Results, It Continues

When motivating employees to change their behavior, remember that positive consequences to any behavior will encourage that behavior, and negative consequences to any

> In explaining the concept of rewards for positive behavior, people sometimes ask about *manipulation*. This word suggests a covert activity, qualities not included in this behavior principle. It's human nature to be interested in self-preservation. But we have needs, desires, and goals that can be met only with the assistance of others. Influencing the behavior of others based on what is pleasing to them and yourself as well is a win-win situation, not manipulation.

"Years have taught me at least one thing and that is not to try to avoid an unpleasant fact, but to grasp it firmly and let the other person observe I am at least treating him fairly."

—BENJAMIN FRANKLIN

behavior are likely to diminish it. The catch is that the consequences must be perceived as positive or negative from the employees' points of view. Too often, supervisors implement consequences that are positive or negative from their points of view and then wonder why the behavior change did not take place. For example, an ongoing issue in manufacturing is the goal of improved safety. In this area, a primary concern is how to motivate employees to wear their safety hats and glasses. The dilemma is that employees perceive more positive consequences for not complying with the policy of safety gear than they do for adhering to it. It is easier, more comfortable, and more convenient to work without hard hat and glasses, so employees avoid them. The supervisory challenge is to motivate employees so that the positive consequences for compliance outweigh the positive consequences for noncompliance.

Consequences That Are Immediate, Personal, and Guaranteed Have Greater Impact Than Those That Come After the Fact

The boss who says, "If you make three $500 sales this week, I'll guarantee you a bonus of $150 to be paid on Friday" motivates the employee more than the boss who says, "If you make some sales this week, maybe I can talk to the

> **"A longing in most of us is a desire to feel appreciated."**

general manager about some sort of bonus for our sales team." On either a conscious or a subconscious level, we assess information to see how it benefits or hinders us. If we recognize the specific benefits of a consequence, then we are more likely to respond with the desired behavior.

The Consequences of Behavior Come From a Variety of Sources

The consequences of behavior can come from a boss, colleagues, subordinates, friends, and the organizational system. They can even come from the job itself. Unfortunately, this makes changing individual behavior difficult. Since there are many sources of consequences, understanding which have the greatest impact on the behavior you want to influence is essential. Frequently, you must work with the person whose behavior you are trying to change in order to discover these.

REINFORCING BEHAVIOR

Rewarding or reinforcing desired behavior is essential if you want a behavior to continue. Do you have a habit of telling others when and why you appreciate them? If you do, you probably are achieving more of your goals than those who don't. There are several ways that you can improve your ability to reinforce positive behavior:

> **"There is only one way to get anybody to do anything. And that is by making the other person want to do it."**
>
> **—DALE CARNEGIE**

• *When people do a good job of reaching a goal, make certain they hear about it.* Employees want to know when they have done well, so talk to your employees when they do a good job. However, also reinforce behavior when something is done better than before. Managers have been heard to say, "I don't need to tell my people that they are doing a good job. They know they are if I'm not chewing them out for something." There is lively discussion when employees are asked if they get enough positive feedback. Usually no more than 10 percent in a group feel they receive adequate positive feedback for a job well done. Most people report that they get far more criticism than positive feedback. What they would like to hear is a sincere compliment when they are doing a good job and reaching desired goals.

> While providing training at a nuclear power plant a few years ago, one of the foremen commented, "You know, one 'aw shucks' knocks out ten 'atta-boys.' " Others nodded in agreement. He continued by saying, "And we don't get enough 'atta-boys' to have ten knocked out. Most of us need to be more positive, and we need to hear more positive words." His remarks underscore the importance of positive feedback as motivation for working toward goals. When we are doing a good job, most of us want to hear about it.

And outstanding performers as well as those who need improvement seek positive feedback. Contrary to some thinking, outstanding performers can be motivated to even higher performance when they know what they do well as well as what they can improve. Additionally, in knowing what they do well, outstanding performers can then educate others to higher standards of performance. Using a performance rating of one through seven, with seven indicating outstanding performance, managers often say, "I never give a seven; no one is perfect." Your response can be, "A seven does not equate with *perfect* performance; it is outstanding performance. And outstanding performers deserve to be recognized." Managers may then argue, "But if you give a seven, employees won't be motivated to try harder." This always has been a weak argument. Outstanding performers generally are motivated to do even better when their performance is exemplary. Not recognizing their performance is a demotivator.

Employees are better able to hear and respond to constructive criticism when there is a balance of criticism and

"One kind word can warm three winter months."

—JAPANESE PROVERB

praise. If an employee hears only the negative, then there is little motivation to improve. The thinking becomes, "Why bother?" Generally, employees want to do a good job and contribute to the organization. Providing feedback, both positive and negative, helps create an atmosphere for improved performance toward established goals.

How often do you take the time to praise others for a job well done?

_____

_____

Do you make a point of providing positive feedback to those who help you accomplish your goals? How frequently?

_____

_____

• *Reward desired behavior immediately after it occurs.* When you reward desired behavior without delay, it has the greatest impact. Your employee is made aware that the reward is the consequence of a particular behavior. His or her attention is then focused on that behavior and its consequence. A colleague who recently switched jobs from one corporate giant to another provides an example. He gave his first major presentation to key members of the corporate staff. Following the presentation, the CEO and his supervisor immediately congratulated him on the presentation. His reaction was one of pleased surprise. At his previous position, his boss might say "good job" sometime following a presentation, but he couldn't count on it and the compliment was often stated in general terms. After experiencing the genuine and timely compliment, he commented, "It sure does help to know what your boss likes."

• *Reinforce the small successes.* Often we wait until employees reach the big goal before we offer meaningful praise. Instead, divide a large goal into several smaller ones so that the intermediate goals seem more achievable, then offer reinforcement along the way. Most of us appreciate periodic reinforcement—it helps motivate us to continue our efforts. When we see the smaller successes accumulate, the momentum and energy build for reaching the final goal. Sincere praise also builds an improved relationship. So look for people who are doing things right. Take a proactive stance and look for successes to reinforce.

• *Be specific in your praise.* Using assertive words, state the behavior that you liked, how you felt about it, and the consequences of that behavior. For example, note the difference between, "Corby, that was a good presentation" versus "Corby, I liked your presentation; it was clear, concise, and well-prepared. I think your ideas will make a difference in the way the engineering manager makes her decision." And finally, affirm the person with a smile or handshake. Your personal warmth often strengthens the reinforcement.

Reinforcing behavior is part of an effective management style. In fact, this is part of the theory of Management by Walking Around (MBWA). One merit of this management style is that you have an opportunity to be on the floor, observing people. It's a rich opportunity to reinforce desirable behavior and correct undesirable behavior.

REINFORCING STATEMENTS

- **Thank you for taking the initiative. . . .**
- **I appreciate your creativity. You enlivened that presentation.**
- **Your appraisal of that assistant was firm but fair.**
- **Your writing is clear and concise. It is easy to follow.**
- **Your efforts to increase efficiency have reduced the work load for all of us.**

POSITIVE FEEDBACK

Suppose last week, you and your staff were responsible for completing a major project. One of your most talented and efficient employees was gone four of the five days, owing to illness. Although he had his own deadlines to meet, another staff member pitched in to help you meet your deadline. Your colleague's cooperation was helpful. What is the positive feedback that you want to give?

CORRECTING BEHAVIOR

> **"If you argue and rankle and contradict, you may achieve a temporary victory—sometimes; but it will be an empty victory because you will never get your opponent's good will."**
>
> **—BENJAMIN FRANKLIN**

For many of us, criticizing what someone else has done comes fairly easily. But effectively correcting behavior takes energy and skill. In fact, correctly identifying the need to correct behavior is a first step. Often, an employee is unable to do as you say or reach a particular goal because he is not ready to accomplish the task for one of the following reasons: (1) the goal is not clearly stated; (2) adequate training or instruction is not provided; or (3) adequate resources (time, equipment, information) are not available. If you do not provide the needed instruction, skill, or resources for employees to accomplish their goals, then it is your responsibility to remedy that situation. However, if the problem is that an employee is not willing to work toward a goal, then you need to correct individual behavior. Effectively correcting that behavior involves several of the methods also discussed for reinforcing behavior.

• *Recognize that correction is part of the feedback process.* This is a necessary and desired part of communication. Most of us want to do well in our work. Effective job performance feedback means hearing when we are doing well (reinforcement) and also hearing when our performance needs improvement (correction). Managers need to provide this feedback for employees and for each other.

• *Correction should occur as soon as possible, but in private.* Each of us has the right to know what we are doing wrong and why, so that we can take steps to improve performance. When correcting employee performance, describe the error specifically, tell what needs to be done differently, and explain why. Although correcting behavior needs to occur as soon as possible following the error, it should be done in private whenever possible. Your intent is to correct for improved performance. If you embarrass, anger, or humiliate an employee, you will lose ground in terms of the relationship as well as performance.

• *When correcting, provide specific feedback.* Use assertive messages and listen carefully. For example, you might say, "I am disappointed that you did not seem prepared for this morning's presentation. Your main points were unclear and your overheads were not relevant to what you were saying. As you know, our goal was to provide the engineering manager with clear, relevant information to aid his budgeting decision for the waste incineration." When providing feedback, express the error, your feelings about it, and provide the consequences of that error.

• *Focus on the error, not the person.* Remember that it is the error (the behavior) that needs correction; the person is still of value to you. When possible, invite input from the individual who has made the mistake. In the previous example, you could ask, "What happened?" or "What can you do to prevent this from happening again?" or "What can you do to remedy this situation?"

Taking the time to ask an individual for input can provide helpful information as to why the error occurred and can help you design steps to prevent it from reoccurring. Asking for input also affirms that you see the employee as a person of value who can contribute to remedying the error. In this way, a learning opportunity emerges from the correcting process.

• *Avoid holding grudges.* The correction process is one of moving forward, not of rehashing old mistakes and holding grudges. Doing so only wastes the precious resources of time, energy, and self-esteem. Develop the personal discipline to forgive mistakes.

You want to correct behavior so that progress toward your goals can continue. These techniques are essential if you want to minimize the frequency and impact of errors. No

---

You are the department head for an administrative group that sometimes experiences bottlenecks as a result of all the paperwork that must be completed. As a result, there are instances of paperwork being completed incorrectly, late, or not at all. To remedy the situation, you have tried yelling, threatening, and publicly denouncing the offenders during staff meetings. You realize that a new approach is warranted. How could you more constructively handle the situation to correct the problem with the paperwork?

TECHNIQUES TO AVOID WHEN CORRECTING BEHAVIOR

- **Losing your temper**
- **Sarcasm**
- **Yelling**
- **Profanity**
- **Public reprimands**
- **Threats**
- **Humiliation**
- **Inconsistent actions**

one is perfect and errors will occur. However, one measure of your effectiveness in motivating employees is the manner in which you correct their mistakes. Effective correction strengthens your authority and the respect that others have for you.

PART

EFFECTIVE GOAL SETTING AND MANAGEMENT SKILLS

CHAPTER 6

SETTING PRIORITIES

How often do you put second things first?

By now you probably have set specific goals for your work, and you have some ideas for accomplishing them. But how do you decide what to do first? A measure of your effectiveness is how skillfully you are able to establish your priorities in order to progress toward your goals. With many responsibilities and activities demanding your attention, you need a way to determine which goals receive the investment of your time and your energy. Only with a practical system for setting priorities will you be able to concentrate on the tasks for reaching your goals. Take a few moments to respond to the priority-setting checklist.

PRIORITY-SETTING CHECKLIST

	Yes	No
1. I set priorities regularly.	____	____
2. I establish priorities on a long-term basis as well as on a short-term basis.	____	____
3. I use criteria to establish my priorities.	____	____
4. I regularly work on the high-priority issues.	____	____
5. I recognize the value of applying my time and energy to the high-priority issues.	____	____
6. I communicate my priorities to others who are affected by my actions.	____	____

A health-care executive faced with many interruptions in the day established a quiet time for himself when he would address priorities. He learned to post a "Do Not Disturb" note on his office door from 7:00 to 9:00 A.M. He then would concentrate on his high-priority tasks, one at a time. The result has been an increasing rate of productivity.

SETTING YOUR PRIORITIES

How do you decide what to do each day? And how do you decide which activities get your attention first? Often we set our priorities in a way tht feels comfortable to us rather than in a way that addresses our goals most effectively. Read these statements and check those that apply to you:

I set my priorities by:

_____ My job description—"I first do what is related to my job."

_____ The squeaky wheel—"Whoever or whatever squeaks the loudest gets my attention."

_____ What my supervisor says to do.

_____ Doing the easy ones first—getting the minor tasks out of the way.

_____ Doing the most difficult ones first.

_____ Last in, first out—the latest issue gets the top priority.

_____ First in, first out—issues are dealt with in the order in which they come.

_____ What is most interesting at the moment.

None of these approaches is optimally effective because none uses a rational, consistent criterion for determining what needs to be done. And without rational criteria to set priorities, you may not work on your most important goals first.

Most people do a reasonably good job of what they do. The question is, Are they doing a good job of those things that need to be done? Frequently, we do not think through what we need to do in order to be maximally effective.

DOING FIRST THINGS FIRST

Problem: You return to your office and find ten telephone messages, and you have only thirty minutes in which to return the calls. *Solution:* Rank the calls in order of importance so you make the high-impact calls first.

A rational system evaluates facts, is easy to use, can incorporate flexible criteria, and is accurate. Remember the 80–20 rule: Of all the things you could be doing to reach your goals, it is likely that about 20 percent of your current effort yields 80 percent of your results. So, there is a good reason to work smarter.

SETTING CRITERIA

An effective method for establishing priorities is to use a table (see Figure 1). The first column identifies your con-

Figure 1.   Table for evaluating concerns by rating the criteria.

Concerns	Criteria	
	Importance	Urgency
1.		
2.		
3.		
4.		
5.		

cerns, which may include your goals, current projects, and activities. Subsequent columns identify criteria to evaluate your concerns.

Criteria often used to rank concerns are importance and urgency. With regard to *importance,* consider the impact of each concern on your goals. Is it an activity of high impact? What impact is likely in terms of cost? Use of resources? What kind of an effect will this activity have on your reaching your goals? As you evaluate your activities using each criterion, assign a number to indicate the level of importance (high = 3, medium = 2, low = 1) and enter this number in the appropriate space of the table.

Follow the same guidelines for evaluating the urgency of a concern. What are its deadlines? Is it a project or goal that requires immediate attention, can it wait for a while, or can it be put aside indefinitely? As you did with the level of importance, assign a number value to indicate the level of urgency for each concern.

There are several thoughts to keep in mind as you use this table. First, people often equate urgency with importance. But the distinction is that importance has to do with impact and urgency has to do with time. Also, remember that each criterion is evaluated on its own merit. As you consider your activities and goals, evaluate their importance and then their urgency relative to each other, considering one concern at a time. For ease, focus, and consistency, limit your criteria to four.

The table in Figure 2 illustrates the method of using criteria to evaluate a list of goals, activities and/or projects.

Rarely are there right and wrong answers, but this method of setting priorities is a defensible systematic strategy for establishing priorities. Once you identify the priority of your activities, you are poised to apply your time and energy to your goals more effectively. Your productivity will sky-rocket!

Figure 2. Sample filled-out table showing the criteria rating method.

Activities	Criteria		Total	Ranking
	Importance	Urgency		
1. You have twenty-four hours to submit a grant proposal.	L=1	H=3	4	4
2. There has been an oil spill.	H=3	H=3	6	1
3. There is a formal complaint against one of your employees regarding sexual harassment.	M=2	L=1	3	7
4. A secretary needs to be hired within thirty days.	M=2	H=3	5	3
5. Complete a time-and-motion study of the productivity in your department.	L=1	L=1	2	8
6. Four of your employees must attend training on sexual harassment two weeks from now.	M=2	M=2	4	5
7. Your CEO will be visiting your plant in one week to tour. His current priorities include adherence to environmental regulations.	H=3	H=3	6	2
8. Six performance appraisals must be completed in the next two months.	M=2	M=2	4	6

Use this method either when establishing individual or group priorities. Even though you are likely to find that your priorities differ from those of others on your team, a systematic review of priorities provides a base of rational thought for supporting your position. When using this method, changes in opinion tend to be driven by facts rather than emotions. Generally you will find reaching agreement quicker and easier through a system that is rationally defensible.

To practice setting priorities, consider the issues, activities, and/or projects that you must deal with in the next week.

Using the table shown in Figure 3, list your issues and concerns, then rank each using the criterion of importance, then of urgency. Total the score and rank your results.

When establishing your criteria, you may decide to use different ones from importance or urgency. The criteria may change depending on what is most relevant to your goals. A key factor in setting priorities successfully is that you are consistent in choosing and applying the criteria.

A group of twenty department heads from a utility company identified twenty-five barriers that were keeping them from working together effectively. They needed to build consensus regarding their five most important issues. The criteria to prioritize each issue was the degree to which each issue: (1) met organizational goals, (2) enabled the productivity of each department head, and (3) enhanced communication of the group. Within three hours the group arrived at a common priority ranking for those issues and initiated planning to address the top concerns.

Figure 3. Table for ranking issues according to criteria rating.

Issues	Criteria		Total	Ranking
	Seriousness	Urgency		
1.				
2.				
3.				
4.				
5.				

YOUR PRIORITIES—
DON'T KEEP THEM A SECRET!

A common complaint among employees is that supervisors do not communicate their priorities. Instead, they assign work and establish goals with little or no apparent rationale. If you take the time to communicate your priorities in relationship to your goals, employees will better understand their role in helping you reach those goals. And your bonus is an improvement in morale!

CHAPTER 7

PLANNING

Without a plan, reaching your goals tends to be a hit-or-miss proposition, and time is easily wasted. Without a plan, you may find yourself reacting to the demands of others rather than focusing on your own goals. Without a plan, you will miss the benefits that come from using effective planning skills. Before considering the benefits of effective planning, perform the self-audit on the next page, and identify your strengths and areas for improvement with regard to planning.

The benefits of effective planning are many. For one, planning leads to higher productivity. Because a plan identifies what needs to be done, by when, and by whom, employees understand their role in accomplishing a specific goal. Arguments over responsibilities, resources, and work schedules diminish. As a result, there are fewer interruptions—employees have the information they need to do their jobs, so they can leave you alone to do yours.

There is also an improved use of resources. With employees understanding their part in reaching a goal, there is less overlap of effort and less time spent in confusion. Consequently, more time and energy are applied to getting results. A fourth benefit is the ability to delegate effectively. With a plan in place to reach your goals, you can identify the tasks to be delegated and the people who can complete them.

It is likely that your employees will enjoy improved morale as a result of your improved planning. Employees appreciate

70

PLANNING SELF-AUDIT

1. How many hours do you spend planning your daily, weekly, or monthly work?   Daily ___   Weekly ___ Monthly ___

2. Do you have a plan for reaching your goals? Yes ___   No ___

3. How many hours are spent managing crises on a daily basis? _____

4. Could some of these crises be averted with planning?   Yes ___   No ___

5. Do you have plans or policies to manage the most frequent concerns and tasks in your department?   Yes ___   No ___

6. Do you set clear goals for yourself? For your employees? (Self) Yes ___   No ___   (Employees) Yes ___   No ___

7. Do you encourage the use of a systematic planning process when trying to reach significant goals?   Yes ___   No ___

8. Do you remember to evaluate your plan in terms of what can go wrong?   Yes ___   No ___

9. Do you have the skills to plan effectively? Yes ___   No ___

"Nothing is easier than being busy and nothing more difficult than being effective."

—R. ALEC MACKENZIE, TIME MANAGEMENT EXPERT

being given a focus, and they appreciate contributing to significant results. Too often, a lack of planning leads to frequent crisis management. And crisis management, with its frantic nature, often contributes to a mismanagement of resources including employees, which leads to a decline in morale. But, in contrast, better planning leads to improved quality. The quality problems that come from rushed or incomplete work are avoided. Systematic planning also helps to identify deviations from what should be occurring, so that you can make corrections before a crisis occurs.

Take a moment to consider your current work situation. What are three benefits of planning that could accrue to you?

_____

_____

_____

PLANNING IS A MANAGEMENT SKILL

Many managers find they become less reactive and more proactive as they increasingly practice effective planning. Instead of embracing a management style that reacts to the crises of the day, planners plan their tomorrows. In the shift from a reactive to a proactive stance, managers find that the number of brushfires they must fight decreases. They anticipate problems and have a plan in place to handle them calmly and systematically.

Planning will help you identify the steps necessary for reaching your goals. In contrast, failing to plan can lead to the perception that you are an ineffective manager. You'll attain fewer results and waste resources because of a lack of planning.

Additionally, conflicts among employees increase because of the confusion that surrounds their jobs. Who is supposed to do what? By when? And for what reason? These are the questions you hear when employees do not have a plan to guide them.

Two additional problems that occur when there isn't sufficient planning are the increased probability of accidents and higher production costs. Inadequate staffing, tight schedules, a lack of resources, and increased time pressures contribute to that higher risk environment. And higher production costs accrue as a result of reduced output, lower morale, and higher stress levels.

"Planning—a rational predetermination of where you want to go and how you intend to get there."

—R. ALEC MACKENZIE, TIME MANAGEMENT EXPERT

Many managers claim that they have no time to plan. Day-to-day events and activities push regular planning into the background. And it's true that fighting brush fires takes time and energy away from fire prevention. However, planning saves time in the long run. Numerous experiments have been made to measure the value of planning. One group applies more time to planning, while a second group goes about business as usual. Repeatedly, the planned work is completed more quickly and with higher quality results.

> Front-line supervisors in a paper mill repeatedly stated that their work load was overwhelming, and that they had no time for planning. The classic response was, "We're too busy fighting fires to plan." Challenged to spend just twenty minutes a day planning, several of the supervisors agreed to give it a try. Within four weeks, those who planned their days found that they were facing fewer production crises and fewer employee conflicts. They also reported feeling more confident about their ability to do their job.

KEY PLANNING STEPS

Six basic questions frame the planning process: Who? What? When? Where? Why? How? Answering these six questions is essential to effective planning. *Who* determines responsibility. It identifies the person responsible for completing each part of the plan. Knowing this enhances teamwork and personal accountability for accomplishing tasks. *What* establishes the goal, and details the results and standards to be met. For example, "Make six widgets" is a goal. But natural questions are, "Can you be more specific?" and "How long do we have to make them?" If you can be more specific, say so. "Make six four-sided blue widgets within the next seven

"If you want people's enthusiasm and motivation for a goal, be clear about your expectations at the beginning."

—DICK HAINES, PRESIDENT, MAYTAG COMPANY

days" is a focused goal. The more specific your goal, the more specific your plan can be. And the clarity of your plan helps diminish confusion, increase confidence, and contribute to the effective use of resources.

When marks the time frame for the plan's beginning and end, as well as providing scheduled progress checks along the way. So for each step, identify the time allotted for completing that step. *Where* identifies the place for carrying out the steps of the plan. *How* defines the steps to be completed, and within each step, clarifies the procedures to be used. Finally, *Why* provides the personal motivation of those involved to work the plan and to reach the goal. Remember that motivation differs depending on the people involved. Take the time to identify what motivates each of your employees to accomplish a particular goal, and then encourage them to use that information.

ENSURING A FAIL-SAFE PLAN

"Develop ownership in your plan with yourself and others, both psychologically and economically when possible."

—WALT SMITH, CEO, THOMBERT, INC.

There are a few more ways you can maximize the benefits of your plan. One is to avoid making assumptions. Be specific—anticipate and answer questions, and document your plan and your progress. Another is to ensure that you look for potential problems in your plan. Parts of your plan are apt to be vulnerable, and these vulnerabilities could disrupt the success of your plan and jeopardize your reaching the goal.

For example, initiating something new creates a vulnerability. If you are doing something for the first time, all the kinks may not have been worked out. Tight deadlines create a vulnerable situation, and so do activities controlled by more than one person. In each situation, consider how you can minimize the potential difficulty.

A third suggestion is to ensure that you communicate with people whose cooperation is essential for the success of the plan. And these people sometimes are different from those who are responsible for carrying out the plan. You will also want to emphasize follow-up and follow-through. Your attention to detail will ensure that nothing falls between the cracks.

Finally, you need to establish a fair method for providing specific feedback to those working the plan, so that praise is given when warranted and correction is provided as needed.

CHAPTER 8

DELEGATING

"My boss says she delegates, I say she dumps."

Which of your responsibilities could be handled by someone else in your organization? How much of the work you do could be delegated to someone else? Of all of the management skills that can have an impact on your effectiveness, delegation is one of the most important. The effective delegator enables achievement of greater results in others. When you delegate projects, you give others authority, responsibility, and accountability.

When you fail to delegate, however, two key problems arise: (1) You handle work that others could do more efficiently and at a lower cost to the organization. (2) You are not investing your time and resources in projects that only you are best prepared to do. In effect, you waste valuable resources of time, money, morale, and energy.

Many managers do not feel comfortable delegating work, however. Delegation is a relatively easy concept to understand, but is difficult to apply. What about you? Are you an effective delegator? Before reading further, consider your attitude and experience by taking the delegation self-audit on the next page.

If you answered yes to ten or more of the questions, then you are well prepared to delegate, and you probably are rarely accused of "dumping" on your direct reports. But if you responded no four or more times, then you are not yet an effective delegator. Developing your delegating skills will enhance your achievement of goals that require the effort and cooperation of others.

DELEGATION SELF-AUDIT

	Yes	No
1. Do you trust your staff to handle job assignments?	___	___
2. Do you avoid being a perfectionist?	___	___
3. Do you give job instructions effectively?	___	___
4. Do you believe that others can do a job as well as you can?	___	___
5. Do you enjoy managing work rather than doing the work?	___	___
6. Do you recognize that making mistakes is part of learning?	___	___
7. Do you follow up with people after delegating?	___	___
8. Do you appreciate the skills and talents of those who work for you?	___	___
9. Do you avoid crisis management?	___	___
10. When you delegate, do you leave your staff alone to do the work that you have assigned?	___	___
11. Do you recognize that delegation is sometimes done in increments rather than as an all-or-nothing proposition?	___	___
12. Do you support your direct reports by your feedback, your actions, and your loyalty?	___	___
13. Do you delegate to the lowest possible level in your organization?	___	___

STRATEGIES FOR BUILDING A DELEGATING ATTITUDE

The delegation self-audit had you consider some ideas that affect your attitude about delegating. Let's take a closer look at these ideas:

1. *Trust your staff.* If you do not trust one or more members of your staff, take time to consider why not. Is he not trustworthy? Is she incapable of handling work that you would like to delegate? Then ask yourself even deeper questions to probe the root cause of your lack of trust:

- Have you provided adequate job instructions?
- Have you provided adequate feedback (positive and negative) about your job performance?
- Have you delegated authority as well as responsibility?
- Do you provide support and build confidence in your people?
- Do you encourage employees to seek you out when there is a question?

2. *Avoid seeking perfection.* That search is futile, and is the cause of misused and wasted resources. Resources applied to a "perfect" project are resources taken away from other projects of value. Instead of striving for perfection, establish a standard of quality and provide a time frame for reaching it. Then let your staff choose any reasonable means to reach that goal.

3. *Understand that giving effective job instructions is related to effective delegation practices.* When you delegate, you may need to provide instructions for completing the job successfully. Explain the assignment clearly, and establish controls for regular feedback. Ensure that your employee understands and accepts the job before assuming that it is delegated and off of your desk.

4. *Recognize that others have the talent and ability to accept and complete assignments.* Sometimes managers do not delegate because they believe that they can complete assignments better than anyone else can. This belief often develops because an employee handles a job differently from the way a supervisor would. Handling the job differently doesn't mean that it is done better or worse, just differently. However, if you and your employee establish the goal to be achieved, the standards to uphold, and a time frame to follow, then the method—within reason—should not matter.

The owner of a retail business once called in a consultant to improve the practical skills of a jewelry repairman who worked in the store. When asked about the problem, the owner said, "The problem is that he doesn't repair jewelry the same way that I do." The owner indicated that he trusted his employee, and that he had the skill to do the work, but that the employee had a different way of doing things. The consultant then asked the owner three questions: Does your repairman complete the repair jobs to the customer's satisfaction? Are you impressed with the quality of his work? Does he complete his work on a timely basis? When the store owner replied yes to these questions, the consultant said, "There isn't a problem with your employee. The problem is your being unable to leave him alone after you have delegated the job to him. The employee is meeting your goal within the required time, and he is satisfying your customers. It doesn't matter that he does the work in a different way than you do. What matters is that he gets the desired results."

5. *Recognize your true interests.* Delegation is difficult for some people because they prefer doing the work rather than managing it. Ironically, people often are promoted to management as a result of their technical excellence, rather than their ability to manage projects and people. If you know that you prefer doing the work rather than planning, organizing, delegating, and controlling a project, then make that known. You do not want to find yourself moved into an area where you must manage other people's work.

6. *Consider delegation a way to teach skills.* Employees are reluctant to accept a delegated responsibility when mistakes are more frequently punished than accepted as part of learn-

"When you fail to reach a significant goal, you become protective, conservative—your self-confidence goes down. These are elements that keep you from reaching your potential and it takes time to work through this. . . . You need to believe that taking risk is acceptable and that mistakes are forgiven."

—WALTER SMITH, PRESIDENT AND CEO OF THOMBERT, INC.

ing. Your willingness to accept mistakes affects the willingness of your staff to accept assignments. Employees must believe that they will be supported for their efforts, even if they do not achieve a goal and/or mistakes are made. The risk of not succeeding is minimized if your delegation is realistic, appropriate resources are provided, and the assignment is understood.

7. *Build in controls to follow up on progress once a project has been delegated.* Those to whom you delegate should be left alone to do the work, but checking on progress is a natural part of management. Build in checkpoints to help identify potential problems so that they can be handled before they become major.

8. *Praise the efforts of your staff.* Praising people's efforts provides important feedback and often motivates continued effort. Your words of praise, a brief note, or a handshake express your appreciation for the skills and talents of your employees. An effective manager shares the spotlight easily and frequently.

9. *Avoid crisis management.* Crisis management impedes delegation. When crises rule, time is not applied to planning, prioritizing, and delegating projects and work assignments related to your goals. When crisis management is at the forefront, delegating the work to reach significant goals

> "Early in our company's history, when someone sold an order, we rang a bell. It quickly became a tradition. We looked forward to hearing the bell for ourselves and for others. It was a simple but effective way to indicate that people were doing a good job. Now that our company is much larger, we use a symbolic bell attached to an engraved walnut base. It is a 'traveling trophy' that continues to symbolize our pride in our employees and their excellent work."—Frank Russell, President, Excellence in Training Corporation

takes a back seat. Avoid crisis management by adhering to established planning schedules and delegating your work.

10. *Avoid reverse delegation.* This situation occurs when an employee returns assigned work to the boss with the expectation that the boss will take it back uncompleted! Use effective delegation practices. Ask questions, expect answers, and assist employees to help ensure that they will complete the work assignments as expected.

11. *Do not use delegation as an all-or-nothing proposition.* Because of varying skills and confidence levels, work often needs to be delegated gradually. As an employee becomes more competent and confident, give him or her more authority with the accompanying accountability.

12. *Support your employees.* Provide the resources and assistance you would expect if you were completing the work assignment yourself. When delegating, your job is to see that the work gets done. Communicate your expectations before the work begins, then tell employees what you expect and what support they can expect.

13. *Delegate to the lowest possible level.* You want to make the best possible use of resources, energy, and knowledge. For example, operating decisions often are best made by people responsible for day-to-day operations. They are the ones with readily available facts and applied experiences. Employees often can contribute to a better operating decision because they are closer to the situation. Delegation to the lowest possible level ensures that you apply your time to the efforts of your position, making you maximally effective.

These thirteen ideas can change your perspective on delegating to your staff. Take a few moments to consider your daily work schedule and then respond to the following questions.

How many hours do you spend (on a daily basis) doing what others could do? _____

What is the dollar cost of that time on a weekly basis? _____

On an annual basis? _____

If you delegate that work, what projects could you now handle to make more effective use of your time?

_____

_____

ACTION STEPS FOR IMPROVED DELEGATING

Can you be a teacher? A coach? A cheerleader? If yes, then you can become a more effective delegator. Six action steps for improved delegating follow. Decide which steps will strengthen your delegation skills:

1. *Select a person whose judgment you trust.* You need to be willing to delegate the task to see the project to its completion. Selecting capable people who get results reflects well on your ability to set goals and make decisions.

2. *Invite input from your staff regarding their interest in and time for projects.* This increases their commitment for the project. In contrast, delegating unilaterally tends to build resentment and discontent.

3. *Offer training when you delegate.* Understand that delegation has a learning curve. People to whom you delegate may need time to develop the knowledge and confidence to handle the task. Delegate at a pace that is fair to the abilities of your staff.

4. *Delegate projects and assignments that are enjoyable.* Don't just give out the tedious or difficult jobs. Employees quickly feel "dumped on" if only the less pleasant projects are delegated. Most of us understand that any job entails dirty work, but we want a reasonable balance.

5. *Delegate a whole project whenever possible.* If a project must be divided, ensure that team members understand how their work contributes to the whole. Without that understanding, they may feel as though they are working in a vacuum, and become less motivated.

6. *Establish your expectations for communication and feed-back*. Encourage employee input. Provide follow-up without giving the feeling you are breathing down their neck. Progress reports help keep everyone on track.

Read the statements that follow and then decide which of the six action steps just introduced is not being followed. Mark your answer by identifying the number of the action step in the space provided.

1. "Why did you add this project to my department? You've already given us enough work for six months. Most of us are working ten-hour days. Why didn't you talk to me before assigning this?" _____

2. "You gave this to me because you hate detail work. Well, I hate it too." _____

3. "This assignment requires drafting expertise. I don't have the background for this. It will take me twice as long to do this as it would take Suzanne." _____

4. "I thought you wanted me to take care of this. If you do, please give me a chance to get it done. We agreed that I would complete this assignment in seven days, but you've been checking on me once a day." _____

5. "I don't know what happened, either. I thought John was supposed to take care of that particular account. It's frustrating to know only bits and pieces about this project." _____

Answers:

1. 2   2. 4   3. 1   4. 6   5. 5

CHAPTER 9

TIME MANAGEMENT

Do you wish that there were more hours in a day? Do you frequently find yourself trying to catch up? Do you feel that time controls you more than you control it? Many of us cry that there is too little time to accomplish all that we would like to do. However, rather than having too little time, the issue may be the way you manage time.

There are strategies that can optimize your use of time so that you can spend more time working toward your goals. For example, ask yourself the following question regularly and thoughtfully: "What is the best use of my time right now with regard to my goals?" Often we function without considering how our time is spent. Questioning yourself about the best use of your time "right now" encourages you to stop and think. You can make a conscious decision about the value of what you are doing. If you plan your time so that you concentrate on those activities that relate to your goals, you raise the probability that you will reach your goals.

Take the time management self-assessment on the next page. Those statements to which you answer no are time-management red flags—areas that, when improved, contribute to more effective use of time.

USING A TIME LOG

How do you manage your time? Do you really know how your time is used? To determine your use of time, record your activities using a time log. Although keeping a running

TIME MANAGEMENT SELF-ASSESSMENT

	Yes	No
1. My goals are written down in a specific, measurable way.	___	___
2. I know the results I want at work for the coming week.	___	___
3. I judge my results by accomplishment, not by level of activity.	___	___
4. I have a system in place to minimize unwanted mail.	___	___
5. I have an effective system in place for reviewing mail, memos, and paperwork.	___	___
6. I attend meetings only if I know the purpose, value, and my contribution to them.	___	___
7. I make it a practice to be prepared when attending meetings.	___	___
8. I look for ways to decrease wasted and unproductive time.	___	___
9. I make a habit of doing the things that need to be done in the right way to avoid mistakes and rework.	___	___
10. I establish time frames for getting my work done.	___	___
11. I use waiting time to get things done.	___	___
12. I can recognize a time waster and take steps to eliminate it.	___	___
13. I listen carefully to optimize communication.	___	___

total of how you use the minutes in a day may not seem appealing initially, the information you'll get about yourself is worth the effort. The time log is a simple but valuable tool for learning more about how you use the hours in your day. When you understand where your time is really going, you can decide how best to invest your hours. Your time log can be a daily calendar divided into fifteen-minute units, or you can use the time log provided below.

Use a time log to track your activities for five business days. Then evaluate the results to find patterns and trends in how

TIME LOG

Date _____

Time	Activity
6:00 A.M.	
6:30 A.M.	
7:00 A.M.	
7:30 A.M.	
8:00 A.M.	
8:30 A.M.	
9:00 A.M.	
9:30 A.M.	
10:00 A.M.	
10:30 A.M.	
11:00 A.M.	
11:30 A.M.	
12:00 P.M.	
12:30 P.M.	
1:00 P.M.	
1:30 P.M.	
2:00 P.M.	
2:30 P.M.	
3:00 P.M.	
3:30 P.M.	
4:00 P.M.	
4:30 P.M.	
5:00 P.M.	
5:30 P.M.	
6:00 P.M.	
6:30 P.M.	

> **"Time is the most valuable thing a man can spend."**
>
> **—DIOGENES LAERTIUS**

you use your time. Some people find that their effectiveness is hampered by interruptions; others are hampered by misguided priorities, an overload of paperwork, unclear assignments, or inefficient and ineffective meetings. Other insights come from the use of a time log. For instance, you may discover blocks of time to which you can apply efforts to accomplish your goals.

PROCRASTINATION

Do you find that there are times when you haven't worked toward one of your goals? Are there some activities that you deliberately avoid? One reason why time slips away is that we tend to procrastinate. Procrastination—it's the "ability" to put off until tomorrow what could be accomplished today. Most of us are guilty of this at one time or another. Unfortunately, over time we become adept at welcoming diversions and at avoiding what needs to be done.

Take a few moments to answer the boxed questions.

I find that I procrastinate because:	Yes	No
The task or project is overwhelming	_____	_____
The task or project is difficult	_____	_____
The task or project is time-consuming	_____	_____
The task or project is unpleasant	_____	_____
The task or project is effort-intensive	_____	_____
The task or project is unrewarding	_____	_____

Although it is unlikely that the tasks you dislike will go away, you can change your behavior and meet the "procrastination challenge." Your self-discipline and the following strategies can help:

- *Identify your motivation for getting started.* For example, you could reward yourself for working for three hours. Or you could remind yourself that the completion of this project will raise your credibility in the eyes of your supervisor. Decide what motivates you and then follow through on it.

- *Ensure that this task or project is a priority.* Use your priority-setting skills to identify the value of work on this project. If it is not a priority, eliminate it from your "to do" list.

- *Break the task or project into its component parts.* This way it is more manageable. Begin by working on just one part of the task.

- *Accept that some projects require a lot of time.* Although we often do not have long blocks of uninterrupted time, we can schedule some time (as we would a meeting) and make some progress on the longer task.

- *Use a ten-minute strategy.* You can commit ten minutes of effort to almost any task. And ten minutes is enough to get you started. If after ten minutes you feel that you must stop, then do. But you may find that you want to keep going after the initial plunge.

- *Reward your effort.* The minutes that you spend procrastinating can be applied to a reward if you just go ahead and take the plunge. The reward may be small, but it can have a high impact on performance. Remember one of the principles of human behavior: We continue to do those things that are rewarding; we stop doing those things that are not.

- *Set deadlines for yourself and meet them.*

- *Avoid absolutes.* Rarely is anything perfect or absolute. Imposing this pressure on yourself impedes progress.

INTERRUPTIONS

If you had a dollar for every time you allowed an interruption in your day, wouldn't you be well on your way to financial independence? Realize that many interruptions are a result of decisions that you make. And a decision to be interrupted may take time away from working on one of your goals. Each time you do not say no—that you pick up your telephone, open your door, or don't communicate that you are busy—you make a decision to be interrupted.

There are several strategies for controlling interruptions. First, refer to your time log and identify those interruptions that seem to occur on a regular basis. If an interruption will contribute to meeting your goal, schedule it to be dealt with at a particular time. More likely you can delegate it to a more appropriate source.

You can also group potential interruptions. For instance, instead of handling telephone calls through the day, have messages taken and then return calls at a designated time of day. To make your telephone calls more productive:

- Avoid social conversation.
- State the goal of the call.
- Put a time limit on your calls.
- Provide a time and number for reaching you if the person you are calling is not available.
- Identify phrases you can use to end your calls politely.

Since another cause of interruption is an open office door, learn to control who steps through it. People who come in to see you generally view the interruption as important—perhaps even urgent. However, the interruption may interfere with activities related to your high-priority goals. Before deciding to accept a visitor, ask for the reason for (goal of) the visit and establish a time limit. If your visitor needs more than ten minutes, suggest a scheduled meeting. Here are five other actions you can take to minimize the impact of drop-in visitors:

1. Don't accept interruptions from people who can have their needs taken care of elsewhere.
2. Do not invite a drop-in visitor to sit down.
3. Do not accept interruptions during your quiet time—this is when you can make progress toward your goals.
4. Establish a policy of encouraging employees and colleagues to schedule appointments when possible.
5. Meet visitors outside of your office.

Consider the following ideas and mark the ones you would be willing to implement as of tomorrow:

1. Begin work fifteen to twenty minutes earlier than you usually do. Getting started even a few minutes early gives you time to mentally prepare for the day.
2. The night before, organize your work for the next day. Identify your priorities, get your desk ready, and think through the next day's accomplishments.
3. Be respectful and courteous of others' time. Limit the interruptions and visits you make to others.
4. Use a clock or a timer to keep you on track.
5. Concentrate on the task at hand. Each time an interruption takes place, you have to stop and then get started again. Efficiency and effectiveness increase when you schedule uninterrupted time for your work.
6. Learn to say no, but be willing to explain your rationale. Doing so saves time in the long run by avoiding assumptions, misunderstandings, and hurt feelings.
7. Plan for essential interruptions. Rarely are circumstances ideal, so build flexibility into your schedule.
8. During work hours, avoid the people who can usurp your time and stay away from places that steal your time.
9. Be assertive. Doing so encourages you to make your own choices and ensures that you communicate them fairly and respectfully.

"Dollars cannot buy yester- day."

—**ADMIRAL HAROLD R. STARK, FORMER CHIEF OF NAVAL OPERATIONS**

Your time is precious. Time spent in unproductive or low-priority activities is a resource taken away from activities that achieve your goals. Managing your time more effectively can help you reach your goals more quickly and efficiently. There is no magic to learning to manage time. It is a simple matter of identifying how your time is currently used, identifying the habits that need to be changed, and applying the strategies to change those habits. The combination of dedication and perseverance, and the application of time-management strategies, will be your key to successful goal achievement.

NOTES

NOTES

NOTES

NOTES

NOTES

NOTES

NOTES

NOTES

NOTES